What Others Are Saying

(T)he sweetness from the crushed flower of your life is so evident in your poetry near the back of *Hope for the Heavy Heart*. I'm keeping it on my desk so I can refer to your poems.

—Joni Eareckson Tada
Author, artist, radio personality, and quadriplegic

This poetry reads like medicine for your soul. Crafted from the journey of physical and emotional pain, Ellen's writing leads you to prayers of honesty and hope. She's living proof that we can do all things through Christ who strengthens us. Thank God for Ellen Richardson and her work.

—Lorna Dueck,
Context TV

We could listen to this all night!

—Youth commenting on a reading of the poetry at a church coffee house

Wind in My Wings

Wind
in My
Wings

A Collection of Poems for the War-Weary

Ellen Richardson

TATE PUBLISHING
AND ENTERPRISES, LLC

This book is designed to provide accurate and authoritative information with regard to the subject matter covered. This information is given with the understanding that neither the author nor Tate Publishing, LLC is engaged in rendering legal, professional advice. Since the details of your situation are fact dependent, you should additionally seek the services of a competent professional.

The opinions expressed by the author are not necessarily those of Tate Publishing, LLC.

Published by Tate Publishing & Enterprises, LLC
127 E. Trade Center Terrace | Mustang, Oklahoma 73064 USA
1.888.361.9473 | www.tatepublishing.com

Tate Publishing is committed to excellence in the publishing industry. The company reflects the philosophy established by the founders, based on Psalm 68:11,

"The Lord gave the word and great was the company of those who published it."

Book design copyright © 2015 by Tate Publishing, LLC. All rights reserved.
Cover design by Joseph Emnace
Interior design by Manolito Bastasa

Published in the United States of America

ISBN: 978-1-68028-384-6
1. Poetry / Subjects & Themes / Inspirational & Religious
2. Poetry / Women Authors
15.02.20

To my dear Dad and to John and Dave,
my closest friends,
who have all been "wind in my wings."

Contents

PART II. ON RELATING TO OTHERS

PART III. ON HOPE IN JESUS

Introduction

This book is so titled because writing it literally gave me "wind in my wings." The majority of these poems were published in my first book, *Hope for the Heavy Heart* in 2008, poems I wrote when I lived in a long-term care facility, in an institution for about two years. When I entered it, I felt little hope that I would leave there in my lifetime, being newly physically disabled after a lengthy, undiagnosed, and untreated severe illness. But God, in His providence and faithfulness, saw fit to help me climb out of the facility; He gave me "wind in my wings" to rise above the institutionalization that had set in (see the movie, *The Shawshank Redemption*). These poems are a testament to the process that God brought me through, the process of healing that took place in my heart as He worked in me.

Please note the Scripture used is taken from the New International Version, the official version of the Bible of the Bible College and Seminary when I attended them.

Hold on to your hats! Let's plunge right in!

PART I

On Emotions

Eternal Love

"God is love,"* pure love
But of an eternal kind
Not love quite as we know it
But unique, you will find

For sometimes what He allows
And what He does†
Causes great pain
Doesn't look anything like love

He uses it to mold you
To draw you to Him
He bids you surrender
And let Him deeply in

He doesn't stop calling
'Til your life is through
He weighs all you are
And all that you do‡

For He wants you to know
Him more deeply, Him more
So you can relate to Him better
When you get to that Heavenly Shore.

---

* "God is love." (1 John 4:16)

† "'For my thoughts are not your thoughts, neither are your ways my ways,' declares the Lord." (Isa. 55:8)

‡ "[H]e [Jesus] will reward each person according to what he has done." (Matt. 16:27b); "[T]he Lord will reward everyone for whatever good he has done." (Eph. 6:8); "[M]an is destined to die once, and after that to face judgment". (Heb. 9:27)

Come Out and Be Strong

Living on the edge
The edge of despair
Climb out of the hole
Only to fall back there

I gain some ground
Then something happens
To plunge me back down deep

To where I struggle
To where I hide
Myself, my dreams out of reach

Where I go to hide
From the dust and the din
Can't feel Him near
Won't let Him in

This is familiar
I know this place
This was my home
Spent years in this space

But do I, do you, when you
Spend extended time here
Stamp on His grace
Instead of drawing near?

We all have bad days
He knows and understands
But try to remember what it's doing
To Him and all of your fans

Discourage them you do
When you choose to live in a shoe
Come out and be strong
You know, it hasn't all gone wrong.

A Heart Full of Love

Open your heart up to His
And you will find there
A heart full of love
To hold your every care

Open your heart
And you will see
That He'll give love
Oh so tenderly

He is the Master
At kindness, at love
Nothing can replace
What comes from above

For He will bestow
On any and everyone
Love true and pure
He asks you just to come

He takes you then
And breaks you down
He crumbles a heart of stone*

He replaces it
With a heart overflowing
With a soft one all His own

A fleshy heart
He will give
He will teach you
To really live

And love in ways divine
Please mold me and take me
Make me wholly thine.

---

* "I will give them an undivided heart and put a new spirit in them; I will remove from them their heart of stone and give them a heart of flesh. Then they will follow my decrees and be careful to keep my laws. They will be my people, and I will be their God." (Ezek. 11:19–20)

Alone and Cold

Alone and cold
That's how I feel

I remember at four
Standing and watching
Violence in our home

That feeling
That alone and cold
Resonates in my being

It stays with me
And comes up
Again and again

There is Your promise
To never leave nor forsake*
But I don't *feel* You
For goodness' sake

Your presence eludes
My pain it exudes
Through each and every pore

And I *feel* all alone
Don't have a home
Feel afraid at my very core

But trust you I must
Must take that leap
And trust in Your Word

For though I may not feel it
I'm really not alone
In my spirit, Jesus be heard.

---

* "He will never leave you nor forsake you" (Deut. 31:6, 8). In context, starting with verse one, Moses is speaking to Israel, saying that he is old and can no longer lead them. He says that the Lord "will cross over ahead of you [Israel]" (Deut. 31:3), and that Joshua will as well. Moses says, "The Lord will deliver them [the kings of the Amorites] to you, and you must do to them all that I have commanded you. Be strong and courageous. Do not be afraid or terrified because of them, for the Lord your God goes with you; he will never leave you nor forsake you." (Deut. 31:5-6). The Scripture goes on:

> Then Moses summoned Joshua and said to him in the presence of all Israel, "Be strong and courageous, for you must go with this people into the land that the Lord swore to their forefathers to give them, and you must divide it among them as their inheritance. The Lord himself goes before you and will be with you; he will never leave you nor forsake you. Do not be afraid; do not be discouraged." (Deut. 31:7-8)

Also Joshua 1:5, "I will never leave you nor forsake you." In context, this is the Lord commissioning Joshua after the death of Moses. The full verse goes like this: God says, "As I was with Moses, so I will be with you; I will never leave you nor forsake you" (Josh. 1:5). But He goes on and this is so powerful:

Be strong and courageous, because you will lead these people to inherit the land I swore to their forefathers to give them. Be strong and very courageous. Be careful to obey all the law my servant Moses gave you; do not turn from it to the right or to the left, that you may be successful wherever you go. Do not let this Book of the Law depart from your mouth; meditate on it day and night, so that you may be careful to do everything written in it. Then you will be prosperous and successful. Have I not commanded you? Be strong and courageous. Do not be terrified; do not be discouraged, for the Lord you God will be with you wherever you go. (Jos.1:6-9)

The Pull of Home

Happy or sad
Good or bad
There is a pull of home for true

Homelife beckons
And it reckons
To be recreated by you

If turmoil you did have
Then unconsciously for real
You may go around
Reliving the same deal

For it's very hard to know
To gain insight, to grow
Not to let the unconscious rule
You need to go to relationship school

For me, it was counseling
That helped me understand
How, for instance, I saw
My father in every single man

I find since turmoil was the norm
That I am at home in a storm
I did cling
To those that sting
As unhealthy relationships I did form

For home has a pull
That's deeper than deep
It'll run your life
It'll play for keeps

So Lord help me
To step out and be
Brave to take the steps
As beyond home I need to get.

Fear

I get in touch with my feelings
Only to see me going under again
I get in touch with my feelings
Only to want to run and then

Fear threatens to grip me
And have me in its vice
I say okay, I'm fearful again
I need some good advice

So I go to God and cry out
To Him, I spill my guts
He listens and advises

He encourages and lifts
My honesty He loves
My sin He despises

"Be still and know
That I am God"*
I sit with Him, my Friend

As He guides me in prayer
He leads me to safety
My wounded heart He does mend

Please free me
Release me from fear's grip
So I do not go reeling
On another trip

A trip designed by Satan
To pull me away
From Him and His grace
And cause me to stray

"We all, like sheep, have gone astray,
each of us has turned to his own way"†
Lord, light my path that I may stay close
May I Your loving, guiding hand know

Free me from fear that threatens to engulf
Let me not give in to Satan's tool
You teach me that You are faithful
Hope and trust You call me to in Your School.

*   Psalm 46:10

†   Isaiah 53:6a

The Eternal Method

God uses ways*
That are all His own
The Eternal Method
Makes us inwardly groan

Groan, "Why?" or
"How could you?"
All the while,
He knows what to do

To make you rich
To make you stand firm
To give you hope
So you won't squirm

Squirm out of your responsibilities
To Him and to others
God gave His Book
And your Sisters and Brothers

To strengthen and to guide
In times of deep pain
His Eternal Method He does employ

Man, how it makes me mad!
How He puts me through things
That me they almost destroy!

Still a mustard seed faith†
Is all that He needs
To grow me up and make

Me rich and blessed
In my *spirit*
He gives but He also may take.‡

---

* "For my thoughts are not your thoughts, neither are
your ways my ways,' declares the Lord." (Isa. 55:8)

† Jesus's words in Matthew 17:20: "I tell you the
truth, if you have faith as small as a mustard seed,
you can say to this mountain, 'Move from here to
there' and it will move. Nothing will be impossible
for you."

‡ "The Lord gave and the Lord has taken away; may the name of the Lord be praised." (Job 1:21) These are Job's words after God allowed the loss of his livestock, his servants and his family.

A Plea in the Grief

So much to let go of
So much is lost
I've regained my mind*
But oh, at what a cost

I feel a deep sorrow
A deep eternal sadness
Wonder if I will again
Live in God's joy† and gladness

Please God help me find
A life worth the living
Help me strike a balance
Between getting and giving

Help me find a place
Where the toil is worth the strain
Help me Lord, get up in the morning
Again and again and again

And say it's okay
Honestly
To find, to hold
Life's key

The key to life, Jesus
He makes it hopeful
Lord, make it
Realistically "copeful"

Please allow me to
Let You find a way
To find meaning and life
In living paralyzed day after day after day.

---

* My mind was severely ill and out of my control for an eleven-month period, during which I made over sixty visits to various emergency departments. Despite this, I did not receive proper treatment in that time span. At the nine-month mark, I went to three different hospitals sharing with them my fears that I would again try to take my life (six months into the mental sickness, I took a near-fatal overdose). In fact, I said at one point that unless I am hospitalized, I intend to jump from the Bloor Street Viaduct, a bridge known for its lethality. Instead of being hospitalized, I was sent twice in one week to a psychiatric crisis center that is, in fact, walking distance from the Viaduct. Two days later after the second visit to the center, I left there on foot, as patients were free to come and go as they pleased. With the illness of the mind untreated and voices constantly tormenting, I walked to the bridge and without hesitation, thinking it was "God's will" for me to do it, leapt off the ledge. I woke up in hospital paralyzed from the waist down, but my mind remained ill. Two months later, I fired my psychiatrist who had behaved incompetently with me, and got a new, more experienced one. This new specialist immediately diagnosed my condition and prescribed the antipsychotic medication I needed all along; my ill mind became well again—a healing that came only after I became paralyzed.

† Three and a half years post-paraplegia, a friend referred to me as "Ellen of Joy."

Angry

In relationship I am
With the Great I Am
Make me frustrated You do
They call it angry too

For you show me things
I just don't get it
They're unfathomable, eternal
Sometimes I want to quit

It's a dynamic relationship
A moving towards and a moving away
And this back and forth
Can change from day to day

Sometimes I'm
Inexplicably in love
Praising You, my Savior
Gratefully gazing above

Sometimes I'm angry,
Even hateful and have disdain
Because you show me things
That cause me great pain

But in the end
You have my freedom in mind
My suffering is for my benefit*
Benefit of an eternal kind.

------

* Just as Jesus's suffering was for my benefit and
bought me eternal salvation, the suffering He
allows in my heart is also for my benefit, making
me a deeper, richer person and preparing me for life
in the hereafter.

Bitterness

It threatens to take you
It threatens to make you
Unforgiving, unyielding, hating, biting

It keeps you from you
It keeps you from me too
It keeps you from wrongs righting

Hate, hate
It cries
Destroy
Despise

It threatens to take your soul
It will swallow you whole
It is a serious enemy
From it, God set us all free

It is a great foe
For it wants your soul to sell
Not the body but the soul
Into a living hell

Where it blocks out
That which is good
For it goes on a mission
Destroy and destroy it could

Destroy relationships
Friends, relatives, loved ones
Get out the knives,
The bullets and the guns

Destroy even yourself
It won't stop at anything
It'll make you its slave
It'll take your wedding ring

It eats away at all that's dear
It'll spread far those that are near
Beware I say beware
To dance extended with it,* don't dare

I think it's part of deep grieving† though
So if you feel it, let it come
But know, it must pass
Into its grasp, you dare not succumb

Let this be a warning then
To you and all you hold dear
Don't hold on to bitterness‡
But to God draw very near.

---

* "See to it that no one misses the grace of God and that no bitter root grows up to cause trouble and defile many." (Heb. 12:15)

† "Each heart knows its own bitterness, and no one else can share its joy." (Prov. 14:10)

‡ "And do not grieve the Holy Spirit of God, with whom you were sealed for the day of redemption. Get rid of all bitterness, rage and anger, brawling

and slander, along with every form of malice. Be kind and compassionate to one another, forgiving each other, just as in Christ God forgave you." (Eph. 4:30–32)

Drunk with Grief

I am drunk with grief
Drunk with despair
Social mores
I don't even care

I sing loudly and long
In the open sanctuary
When no one is there

I say to the crucifix
On the wall, "F—you"
In full humanity, I do even dare

For I'm angry and bitter*
Bitter as can be
My blood boils over
It rages inside of me

I tried to find Home
My eternal one and true
Because my earthly one
Just wouldn't do

I hope there will come a time
When I'll be able to say
I've learned a lot, it makes some sense†
And live for Judgment Day

When all will be made clear
Was it my fault or theirs?
And once again I'll walk
Finally free of my paraplegic cares.

---

* I got over my rage and bitterness with good counseling.

† Six years or so after writing this poem, I could honestly say I've seen suffering that I never before had imagined existed, and by that time as well had the privilege of helping over forty people come to faith in Jesus.

O Selfish God?

What a God
But a selfish one
Would take most of my life
Then ask me to go on?

He didn't save me, it seems
Or provide a way out
When all that was within me
Was bitter rage and doubt

The bitter rage persisted
Was as strong as it could be
Anger so vile
Deep inside of me

Anger for them
And for myself too
I hardly escaped
My inner wrath for true

For I killed myself
Or at least did try
A strong Christian too
Some say, "My, my, my."

Satan gets us down
And wants us to stay
In despair so long

He plants in our hearts
Seeds of destruction
That *feel* so strong

With illness of the mind
Recurring and relentless
To these *feelings*
We can *feel* defenseless

But just know that
Satan is a defeated foe
God can forge
Out of deep despair hope

For a human spirit
Is resilient for true
God is really there
For me and for you

To take all that's precious
And ask me to go on
Seems to me selfish though
Or could I be wrong?

What kind of love
Is that which requires
A stripping of all
That one hopes or desires?

A revamping of life
A restructuring too
Hopes and dreams revisited
He makes everything new*

Can I possibly say
That He knows what He's doing
Can I really just trust?

One sweet day
He'll make all things clear
Cling to the hope of that Day[†] I must.

---

*   "He who was seated on the throne said, 'I am making everything new!'" (Rev. 21:5)

†   Referring to Judgment Day in Hebrews 9:27: "[M]an is destined to die once, and after that to face judgment".

Vulnerability

No one should be paralyzed
With this world being as it is
Fraught with anguish and pain

They say, "Life is difficult"
Even without the paralysis
Now it's doubly so and again

"Life is complicated"
"Life is unfair"
Now I have to live it
From this chair

Can't get around
Like I used to do
Can't relate so easily
From me to you

A social barrier
I find this wheelchair to be
Do you cringe deep inside
When you see me?

Do I remind you
Of your brokenness inside?
You know, the part of you
You always try to hide

No one should be paralyzed
But could it possibly be
That I am like this so you can see
Your own deep and fragile vulnerability?

Isolation

Raised in a space
Where I did not
Feel part of the human race

Where connection
Was lacking and
So was any real direction

Didn't bond well
With my folks,
Satan, towards evil
He did coax

For me, it was suicide
That he impressed upon me
He said that if I did it
I could be "free"

"Free" from worldly torment
And the things that got me down
That it would promise to relieve me
Of my constant and perpetual frown

And it caused me
To further isolate
A downward spiral
It did precipitate

I sunk deeper and deeper
Into my own little world
Until it grew so large
That I was overwhelmed

And attacked to such an extent
That it seemed like the only option
The very best thing to do

Watch it
'Cause Satan can
Do the same to you

He is tricky and powerful
A formidable foe
Jesus had to die so agonizingly
To right Satan's wrong, don't you know

Isolation he uses
To pull you from the things
That can strengthen, give hope

The devil will pull you
From others to himself
Take you to the end of your rope

Then the temptations begin
Be very careful
Of this one called Satan

For he will urge you to do
Things you normally wouldn't do
Beware of isolation, his tool
To get you to harm yourself and others too.

A Feeling of Power

There is a feeling of power
That I received as a youngster
Growing up in the home I did

My Mom asked me to be
Caretaker, counselor,
And in those roles I hid

Wow! To be smart enough
And brave enough too
To instruct my own mother
And tell her what to do!

Gave me an awesome sense
Of power, of control
Gave me the illusion
That I was in control

Gave me a feeling too
That I could do anything
If I could to my Mom
Support and comfort bring

I never did realize
Until this very day
That that feeling of power
Has lead me astray

It has produced in me
Almost "delusions" of grandeur
Thinking myself great
And all others as insecure

Bring me back to earth, Lord
Help me to see
That You alone are Great

Help me to embrace others
Not considering myself superior
And from them, not isolate.

PART II

On Relating to Others

Paralysis of the Will

I have a friend
Who's stuck in a rut
Deeply burrowed down

He can't find his way
He's wrapped in chains
Feels trapped within a frown

For he carries with him
Bag upon bag of care
In his unconscious
It's deeply hidden there

Just out of reach
Just out of view
God take him
On a way that's new

'Cause the weight of that baggage
It paralyzes his will
We try to help
But he persists still

In carrying his luggage
Not unloading and unpacking it
He's working so hard
He just won't quit

So help him surrender
It all, Lord, to You
So You can shoulder
And carry it too

For he's too strong to be weak
Oh help him to see
That You and I he needs
To live interdependently.

Separate

I am separate
From the one I love
I feel so unbearably sad

For me to tolerate
My deep aloneness
You come in and live inside

And you say that
You will never leave
Nor forsake me ever

Thank you that you stay
Right next to my broken heart
For it needs you so

For in my pain, I am prone
To wander, to stray
Help me cling to You, Jesus my Comfort
With all my might, today.

Ode to Jack

Burdened with a family
That don't know how to care
About the things that move Jack's heart
They really don't dare…

…dare to enter in
They stay on the sidelines
He's a psych. patient
That is his crime

They live in caves hiding
Live in busyness striving
Not offering a hand to hold
Inside they are distant, cold

For he is a mental patient
To them and always will be
Debilitated, struck down
Vulnerable and weak

Look down on him they do
As an equal he's not seen
In a psych. ward and a mental hospital
That's where he's been

So he's judged
For this illness of his
Not of his own making
But of God's, it is

Yet on solid ground
Jack stands on the Rock*
He seeks help from His Creator
And from his trusted doc

He works things through
When he gets tired or overwhelmed
He knows where to go
For help in the psychiatric realm

He's braver than he knows
He takes his illness and grows
He talks about his feelings too
All the right things he does do

Jack may be your neighbor
He's not so far from you
So look upon this man named Jack
You might just learn a thing or two

Think twice when you
Cross him on the street
He is truly amongst the most
Honorable men you could meet.

---

* See Isaiah 26:4: "Trust in the Lord forever, for the Lord, the Lord, is the Rock eternal."

A Connection

They work in the institution
And every day they find
Overwhelming needs

Each day they come
Many can do little more
Than the basic physical deeds

Many come in and out
Just doing the physical task
They cannot engage with me
I have to wear a mask

A mask that says I'm okay
They don't talk with me today
Their minds are so full
Of their own aches and pains

Because the needs in this place
Are so overwhelmingly huge
Some find it hard to smile
And face the day as new

For I am the needy
Am I spurned too?
Spurned for my vulnerability
I touch a part in them I do

That part in them
That makes them feel small
That part in them
That they find hard to tolerate at all

My dear caregivers
I really do thank you
For what you do for me

But won't you please try
To make a connection
Wouldn't we then both feel more human, more free?

An Abandoning Person

"Weak one,
I find you too much
I cannot reach out
Your heart to touch

For you trigger something deep inside
That I just cannot stand
The little person in me
That makes me feel less of a woman, less of a man

I want to engage
But deep down within
I can't get it right
I really can't win

Try to forgive
I know that you can
I've tried my best
Try to understand

But go I must
And go I will
I know you need me
I have to go still."

Lukewarm

Wear it 'round your neck
For everyone to see
Wear it on your arm
With your heart on your sleeve?

Or keep your feelings in tight
Never digging deep to say
That pain that you keep hidden
Find it hard to articulate?

"Come to me but go away
In my heart you cannot stay
Have no room for you
For my hurts I cherish I do

I cling to my hurts
They serve me well
The definition of strong
Is not to talk or to tell"

But I say to you that
Into the hands of God
Is where these hurts really belong

To bring them forward
And to face them
Is what truly makes you strong

That would give God
A chance to make it right
You could give Him your hurts
Instead of holding them tight

"I just though seem to sit
On a fence between hot and cold
Can't take that step of faith
Days pass and I grow old

Lukewarm* I guess I am
I guess I do need to grow
Beyond this fence
I see now I need to go."

* Jesus's words in Revelation 3:16: "So, because you are lukewarm—neither hot nor cold—I am about to spit you out of my mouth."

Facing Myself

Facing myself
It's the hardest thing
To hear the music
And let it sing

Not just hearing
But listening too, you see
To all that's going on
Inside of me

I find I cannot know
Trust me, it's true
What is underneath the surface

Until I let
Someone in
To help me handle the mess

The mess that is pain
The mess that is rage
I needed godly counsel
In order to turn the page

To go from pain to peace
To find some resolution
Seeking a Christian counselor
Has been a real solution

For facing myself
And the hurt deep within
Is so difficult, takes God
To keep me from sin

Lord, I don't want the rage
To come out in other ways
As it comes up, help me face it
And not run away and quit

Let me be brave then
And step out
I can find freedom with help
That I won't doubt.

My Former Psychiatrist

You didn't take me seriously
When I wanted to die
So once with pills
And with a jump I did try

'Cause voices I was hearing
And I did tell you so
You didn't believe me
Maybe now you know

Into a pit
Of deep despair
You let me go
You didn't seem to care

For so many months
Psychotic you did leave me
Though I had just a few years prior
Earned an MDiv and a BRE

I want you to know
That I am hurting so
And it's only through Jesus's blood
That I can wade through this mud

And find forgiveness
In my soul
Forgive "77 times"*
Is what I'm told

So I will pray for you
And I will pray for me too
To let you go into the hands
Of a righteous God as before Him
You'll have to stand.

---

* "Then Peter came to Jesus and asked, 'Lord, how many times shall I forgive my brother when he sins against me? Up to seven times?' Jesus answered, 'I tell you, not seven times, but seventy-seven times.'" (Matt. 18:21–22)

Ode to the Nurses

Such difficult work
Is what you do
Cleaning up messes
That we leave for you

You persevere
Even despite
Difficult patients
That test your might

Some of us do
Test you it's true
For we have so many needs

But thanks I do say
And applaud you today
For I couldn't do without you, indeed.

Six Arms and As Many Legs: Ode to the Nurses

"Six arms and as many legs
Is what I feel I need
To accomplish the task
That God sets before me

I have a good day
When most things go okay
But there are days when
So much goes wrong and then

Then I want to scream
Or maybe have a good cry
Stocks are low or out
And the in-charge makes me sigh

At home too I have
Troubles that are real
Hard not to bring
Them to work I feel

In many directions
I'm being pulled
Sometimes, for true

God help me
Keep it together
To serve people, to serve You."

Sour

I look at one nurse's face
And all I see is sour
I hear your voice
And inside I can cower

For your anger you use
As a weapon, as a tool
To keep me quiet
Make me your fool

But deep down inside
I remember a mum
Who filled with anger
Would make me dumb

Quiet and silent
Unable to assert
Myself, my responses
Would tend to be curt

For inside I recoiled in fear
From her anger and rage
My stomach all in a knot
Me unable to turn the page

Because as a child, I felt
So stuck in the pain
Not able to rise above
And see the Son once again

And now I'm prone
To be triggered by
An angry nurse
And in pain I lie

Lie there for a bit
But I don't get stuck as much
Because indeed it is a sad person
Who belittles the vulnerable and such

Jesus helps me now to see
That she was mislead
Rage and hurt she herself
As a young one was likely fed

So I can forgive
And reach down a hand
As God has done to me
To help her to stand.

Denial

Denial is a demon
That takes you away
It keeps you in a box
Out of touch, in the gray

It seems to protect you
From the nasty truth
That you just can't seem to face

But truth is truth
Nonetheless, it marches on
Regardless, from day to day

It knocks now and then
To try to gain entrance
Into your troubled heart

If you would but listen
And let it in more
Then we could make a start

But as it is you sit
In denial strong
And I stay impotent and sad

You won't let me help
Independence your god
It's all you've ever known or had

Now what you need
Is interdependence
To break the barriers down

Can we work together
On this problem so big?
I know a solution can eventually be found.

Just Like You

Don'cha know
I'm just like you?

I may be disabled
Look different too
But don'cha know
I'm just like you

I live in a wheelchair
From a spinal cord injury
Aside from this
You're no different than me

I suffer like you do
I rejoice like you too
I dare to dream as well

About a spouse
About a house
About excitement to tell

And I dream of friends
Of people who reach out
Beyond the metal frame

To see that I have
So much to offer
Though I may be lame

I hurt just like you
When people bypass me
Sometimes I wish I could
From this wheelchair be free

But this is my cross
You have one too
Don'cha know
I'm just like you.

Contagious

Contagious
It's outrageous
But oh so true

Evil and goodness
All of it no less
Has a ripple effect from me to you

For good promotes good
When you witness true love
You'll want to know
What those folk are made of

With evil
Well, it's the same
With evil
It's no game

A complaining spirit
Is like a damp cloth
That spreads all around

WIND IN MY WINGS

Gossip can lead to more
And before you know it
Someone is literally torn down

With suicide, there's a ripple effect
If a crack in the foundation you do detect
It can lead to all crumbling down
Result in rubble right to the ground

Remember that suicide does leave
A trail of folk who grieve
And it really could inspire
Another to suicide, to conspire

I know you may be
In unrelenting pain
Know we are blessed though
By your movement forward again

So what I am saying is this
Remember that in what you do
People are watching and waiting
They might follow your example good or bad too.

PART III

On Hope in Jesus

Turn and Trust

Turn and trust
The Savior true
For He really wants
You, yes you

You need to acknowledge
This problem called sin
You need to say yes
And let Jesus in

For He paid the price
He paid it in full
The penalty for your sin and mine

And He does forgive
No matter what
Time after time after time

Just say, "Jesus come in
Be the Lord of my soul
Forgive my sins, please make
Serving you my true goal"

For being holy
He cannot abide
By the sin in your heart
That you try to hide

So give it to Him
Give Him your life, too
'Cause He freely gave His
For me and for you

Do it now, my friend
You know you really must
To be right with a holy God
You need to but turn and trust.

Deep, Deep Love

I get really scared sometimes
And I wonder whether
I can make this paraplegia fly

I wonder whether
I'll find and keep hope*
I wonder if I could go that high

And I wonder if I will find
True love again in my life
One who could embrace
Me and my disability strife

But in the meantime
I will go and build
On the friendships I have
And from You be filled

For I know that You love me
Through many and much
My family, my friends
Circumstances and such

You melt away the fear
And make me bold again
As I feel deep, deep love
From You, Jesus my friend.

---

* Five years post-injury, I am preaching, leading and coordinating an Adult Sunday school class, leading group therapy, and co-facilitating a depression/manic-depression support group.

Leaning on Christ

This is a terrible, wonderful thing
To lean wholly on my Savior
There are so many other things
That try to draw me in

Money tempts me to cling to it
So do the structures around me
I know that You alone keep my world
From crumbling into dust

Tsunamis, earthquakes, hurricanes
You have at your beck and call
One word from You and
You could take it all

My health too lies precariously
In Your hands for true
I cannot make it an idol
For You could take it too

So trust You I will
I'll cleave to You still
For that is the only way

To preserve my peace
For You never cease
To give me Your strength just for today.*

---

* Jesus's words in Matthew 6:34: "[D]o not worry about tomorrow, for tomorrow will worry about itself. Each day has enough trouble of its own."

A Prayer about Food: A Tempting Panacea to Stress

"Dear Lord:
You know how I struggle
When things go wrong
Can give in to food
Can't seem to stay strong

God's diet plan
Is discipline, or so
Charles Stanley has said

But in stress, I can reach
For sweets, for goodies
Foregoing discipline instead

I need Your strength to resist
Satan's tempting spread
That which is so readily available

In this culture I have
Though others have not
Please make me capable

Of thinking more globally
And not just of myself
With Your help, those cookies
Will stay on the shelf. Amen."

Flowers in the Desert

I have a little cactus
All prickly and tough
Bristles and leather skin
That's what it's made of

On its surface
Grow star-shaped thorns
All symmetrical, each one
Growing from a single skin horn

But it's exterior betrays it
For from deep down within
Spring nine pink blossoms
From deep beneath the prickly skin

Nine radiant blossoms
In all pink, yellow and white
It really is
Quite a delightful sight*

I am a little cactus[†]
All prickly and tough
But from deep down within
Surprisingly grow prettiness and beauty and such

Such like I've never known
Or could never believe to be
Out of a barren desert
A spiritual loveliness grows in me[‡]

So if you're dry
Just know
That spiritual
Flowers can grow

Where and when
You least expect
The creator of Whom
May be God I suspect.[§]

---

[*]   This was an actual plant that I bought at a small store
    near the institution.

† I felt as though, living in the institution, I had developed a "thick, prickly" exterior.

‡ "If I do say so myself...!" (Something I couldn't help but notice...)

§ This was written about eleven months after my injury when I had some doubt about the very existence of a loving God.

Harder to Hold

It's getting increasingly
Harder to hold
On to Your hand*

Cruelty of thought and deed
From ones who claim to be
My very brothers in Christ

Abandonment of Scripture
Their hearts backslidden
Indeed hardened, turned away

They fail to see
And cannot abide by the conviction
Of the very Holy Spirit
That breathes life and love into me

They turn from the face of God
I cannot just stand by
God redeem them, enlighten them
To the wickedness of their ways

You have taught us to
Pray for those who persecute
"Love your enemies, and pray
For those who persecute you"†

This behavior drives me
I find, to demand answers
To the questions I thought
You and I had resolved

It's getting increasingly
Harder to hold
On to Your hand

Where else can I go
But to You, so help me Lord
Strengthen my grasp
Don't let me slip.

---

* This was written when I was out of the institu-
tion and felt betrayed by people I thought were
good friends.

† Jesus's words in Matthew 5:44.

Our Power Source

Just like the TV
Needs to be
Plugged in to work

Just like the nerves
In my limbs need to be
Connected to the
Spinal cord to function

Just like the branch
Needs to be
Attached to the vine
To receive nutrients and live

So we need to be
Connected to Jesus
For the Holy Spirit
To abide in us

For God is our Power Source
We need to remain in Jesus*
For Him to be able
To produce fruit in us

So please get and stay connected
To Our Creator†
Surrender and let the Spirit
Take full control.

---

* "I am the vine; you are the branches. If a man remains in me and I in him, he will bear much fruit; apart from me you can do nothing." (John 15:5)

† "For by him all things were created: things in heaven and on earth, visible and invisible, whether thrones or powers or rulers or authorities; all things were created by him and for him. He is before all things, and in him all things hold together." (Col. 1:16–17)

Tunes

What frequency are you on?
What tunes do you listen to?
Do you tune into the Spirit?
Is there God's flow in you?

Do you hum a God song
As you go along your way?
Do you listen to Him
What He wants and tries to say?

Or do you let the noise
Of the world distract and diffuse
Maybe even noise as a
Buffer from God you use

For God can tell us
And show us things
That cause us great pain

To stay with Him
And ride it out
Can bring us, though, ultimately great gain

But it can be tempting
To veer away
To get caught up
In the world's way

As Danny Brooks does sing
Please, Lord, "Fence Me In"
I want to stay in the flow
And hear Your tunes within.

Frozen in the Snow

I stand here in this pain
Just frozen in the snow
I feel terror on every side
Don't know which way to go

I go back to when
I would want to go to them
My mother, my Dad
My family all make me sad

For I think of my Mom
And terror I remember
Approaching her then
Fury unleashed

For what and why
I never could understand
I know it made me feel little
Made me feel I was to blame

With my Dad, the same
Fury unleashed so easily
I could never be right or good
It seemed, just being me

My family? They scapegoated too
Made me feel shame
I would sit at the dinner table
And the accusations they came

I learned to hate people
To hate myself and life
I saw it as loveless and comfortless
Nothing but stress and strife

Now God calls me
To embrace my pain
To work it through
Again and again and again

As I have learned
To let God be God
That He is "I Am"
And that I am not

A love for people
He has replaced for the hate
Only He could do it
Only He is that Great

Only He could do it
I could not have changed
Like that on my own

His love, He has infused
He has showered
He has shown

And I have embraced
The love as well
Foreign though it is
I have praise to tell

Oh, I so give thanks
For my Savior inside
Who is my Strength,
My Hope and My Guide.

A Spiritual Suicide

When I say
"Don't give up"
What does come to mind?

You think perhaps
Of the ultimate
"Giving up"—you think of suicide.

But let me say
That there are ways
Of giving up for true

That do not involve
A made resolve
To end the life that's you

For you can give up and remain
In the very flesh that you call home
You can abandon Christ
And let yourself freely roam

Roam into waywardness
Roam into sin
Won't come near Jesus
Won't let Him deeply in

"For I want a way
That is my very own
Don't want Jesus
To in me make His home

I want what I want
Nothing else will do
You can let Jesus lead
That's okay for you

Jesus's way is too tough
This I must forfeit
I won't do what He asks
I can't, I just quit"

Give up on God
While living in your skin?
Choosing your own sweet way?

Oh, please, this is a death
A spiritual suicide!
Won't you turn back to Him, now, today?

Clinging to Him
In this world of care
Is the only sure way
There, there, there…

Please find it in yourself
To face Him once again
For He longs to commune with you
And be an everlasting Friend.

Sharpness: The Result of Courage

Lately I've been
So burdened with care
That I retreated

Into sleep
Into laziness
Kind of felt defeated

Wanted to ignore
All the trouble for sure
Felt like facing it
Wasn't the cure

But when finally
I did get up and go
I realized I was dulled
By that laziness, you know

For there is a sharpness
That comes when we face
Our pain, our trials head on

To make the decision
To retreat, I think
I may have been wrong

We all get tired
And are tempted to give in
Help me though
Not to involve sin

Slothfulness doesn't fit
Me as a child of God
I do know my courage
You, Jesus quietly applaud.

Spiritual Obesity

Spiritual obesity*
I see it everywhere
People living in a way that
They really don't care

Don't care for their neighbor
Don't care for themselves
They leave good nutrition
And exercise on the shelf

Hoarding the carnal
And things that they lust
No room for God
No room for trust

Wasting time on the frivolous
Talking, not saying much
Wallowing in self-pity
Blaming and such

I feel so sad
When I see someone
In this state

Open their eyes
Show Yourself
To be the One who's Great

Great at love
And wisdom too
All they need
Is to give their heart to You

For You transform
The self-loathing
The shame, the pain

Into peace
And freedom
And hope once again

Wind in My Wings

So free up souls
Who are caught in a mire
Set hearts ablaze
Set them on fire.

Time

Time proceeds
Relentlessly

It forges on
Through a storm
Through the rain
With the sun

It doesn't stop
For hurricanes
For earthquakes
For natural and
Personal disasters

It doesn't stop
When the integrity
Of our bodies fail

It plows right along
Through weddings
Through funerals
It is no respecter of events

Seems like the more we enjoy
The faster it goes
And when we want it to speed up
It crawls at a snail's pace

Time can be
Glorious friend
Or hated foe

Especially in the afterlife
Depends on
To which place you will go

Though time is relentless
It'll come to an end
Time as we know it
We will all but spend

Eternal—I can't fathom
But that's the deal
Our souls, ourselves
Will spend it somewhere

And on a decision*
It will all hinge
Whether we will go on
In torment or bliss

"Turn and trust"
I've said it before
Surrender your heart
Into His.

---

* "[I]f you confess with your mouth, 'Jesus is Lord,' and believe in your heart that God raised him from the dead, you will be saved." (Rom. 10:9); "Jesus declared, 'I tell you the truth, no one can see the kingdom of God unless he is born again (or born from above)." (John 3:3)

When I felt Jesus lift a great heavy burden—the burden of the scapegoating I endured as a child—off me on a new level, I wrote a trilogy of poems about freedom. Here they are:

Sweet Freeing Jesus

Sweet freeing Jesus
You make my heart sing
Close to Your breast
Forever will I cling

I am so glad
To be able to say
That I love you more dearly
Than ever today

For you free me from chains
And fetters so strong
You knew it was wrong for me
To live with them on

You helped me shout, "Freedom!"
And throw them aside
Near by your side
You ask me to abide

For relentless is evil
So relentless I'll be
To find hope, to find love
To know what it is to be free

Thank you, dear Savior
For helping me see
That I was meant for You
And You were meant for me.

Flying with Jesus

Flying I do
I float like a bird
Soaring high above
Singing songs yet unheard

Flying I feel free
And truly happy
Didn't know, wouldn't believe
That such freedom I could receive

You heal me you do
I know that it's true
And I'll never be the same

Thank you for mending
Thank you for sending
Jesus—truly the name above any other name.

Jesus Frees Us

Jesus frees us
Sends us soaring
To heights and special places

He kindles and rekindles
The fire within and
Brings us into wide open spaces

Where He can show us
The truth of who we are
As individuals, as Christians
He brings near what was far

Far out of reach
Or so I thought
To search in and up
Is what He's taught

I really cannot say
Nor adequately put into words
All that I feel
All that I've heard

Heard from Jesus
As He teaches me His way
With Him forever
I believe I will stay.

Routine

I live in a world of routine
Where regimentation rules
But that, in fact, can be seen
As the very tool

That God uses to produce
Endurance of spirit and faith
Endurance of heart
A toughness it makes

Resiliency of spirit
Not hardness though
He makes you a conduit
As you let His love flow

You need to know
And be able to discern
What to take, when to say no
You really need to learn

To let in and let out
Just like a breath
Take in the good
And discard the rest

Routine is there, yes
But we need a balance to strike
Between work and play
Between fun and strife

A balanced routine
That's how we become
A diamond—it's coal under pressure

A flower will wilt
And eventually give way
To fruit, then seed that is hidden treasure

And from a single seed
Many more can come
So let go and let God work
Right 'til He's done

For it is through
Structure and healthy routine
That perseverance, character
And hope* can be seen.

---

*   "[W]e also rejoice in our sufferings [relentless rou-
tine may be seen as "sufferings"], because we know
that suffering produces perseverance; perseverance,
character; and character, hope." (Rom. 5:3)

Love Affair

You say you are not in love
But I beg to differ
You are in a love affair
Of one sort or another

Is it independence, is it fear?
Is it the bottle, or the drugs?
Is it tobacco or is it caffeine?
Or is it another in codependence?

Loving is who we are as humans
It's what we share, it's what we crave
But I caution you
Not to cling to anything...

...or anyone more than
You do to Jesus
Choose Jesus to adore
Make Him first I implore

Let Him carry
Your trials
Even yourself
As in "Footprints"*

A faithful God
He really is
But you must choose with whom/with what
You have your greatest love affair.

Love[†] and receive Him
The Creator of your soul
And He will, in turn, give to you
Riches[‡] untold.

---

* "Footprints" is the most famous bit of prose by Margaret Fishback Powers:

> One night I dreamed a dream.
> I was walking along the beach with my Lord. Across the dark sky flashed scenes from my life. For each scene, I noticed two

sets of footprints in the sand, one belonging to me and one to my Lord.

When the last scene of my life shot before me I looked back at the footprints in the sand. There was only one set of footprints. I realized that this was at the lowest and saddest times of my life. This always bothered me and I questioned the Lord about my dilemma.

"Lord, You told me when I decided to follow You, You would walk and talk with me all the way. But I'm aware that during the most troublesome times of my life there is only one set of footprints. I just don't understand why, when I need You most, You leave me."

He whispered, "My precious child, I love you and will never leave you, never, ever, during your trials and testings. When you saw only one set of footprints, it was then that I carried you."

† The first of the Ten Commandments, Deut.5:7: "You shall have no other gods before me". Jesus's

words in Matt.22:37-38: "Love the Lord your God with all your heart and with all your soul and with all your mind. This is the first and greatest commandment."

‡ Not necessarily riches of the material kind, but spiritually, as in salvation and as in fruits of the Spirit: "love, joy, peace, forbearance, kindness, goodness, faithfulness, gentleness and self-control" (Gal. 5:22–23a).

Choosing Real Life

"We pause for just a moment
To honor the fallen
On this Remembrance Day*

We interrupt this program
To bring you a few images
Of war and of its way

Way of destruction
Of horror, of terror
Please tolerate and stay

Stay on this channel
Just for a moment
Then we return you
To your regular show

To that which makes
You feel better,
Feel comfortable
You are free to go"

I say I choose
Real life

I choose to recall
The horror, the strife

Not only of war,
But of all the hell
That is on this dark earth
Dark stories to tell

Of abuse, of rape
Of incest, of greed
And all of the sins from which
We can be freed

I don't live in the hell
But touch it I will
My Savior comforts and loves
My heart is filled

For it was for real life
To defeat the prince of this world
That Jesus died and rose again
To the real hell, Satan was hurled.

Praise Jesus,
The One, the Only
His Life, His Light

Makes it possible to face real life
Including the devil, his demons
And all their diabolical might.

_____

* Written November 11, 2011.

A Gentleman

He is a gentleman
He doesn't take over and step in
He asks us merely to come
Come and follow Him

He gently leads
So quietly and softly too
He does it so tenderly
Look! He even calls you!

He will not force
Himself upon anyone
But He doesn't stop calling
'Til your life is done

For suffering and dying
Are yet but tools
He uses to draw you near

To break down anger
To fill you with wonder
To help you face your deepest fear

Deep suffering
A precious gift
With it He does
Want to lift

Lift you up
To higher ground
With Him is where you belong

That's why it urges
In Scripture time and again
Be courageous and be strong*

For Jesus is a gentleman
He only whispers to you
He asks you to listen
And then obey Him too

You can choose
To go your own sweet way
But you reap what you sow[†]
Both now and on Judgment Day.[‡]

---

[*] Deut. 31:6, 7, 23: Josh. 1:7, 9, 18; 10:25: 1 Chron. 22:13, 20; 28:20: 2 Chron. 32:7

[†] "A man reaps what he sows." (Gal. 6:7); "Remember this: whoever sows sparingly will also reap sparingly, and whoever sows generously will also reap generously." (2 Cor. 9:6)

[‡] "For God will bring every deed into judgment, including every hidden thing, whether it is good or evil" (Eccles. 12:14); "[M]an is destined to die once, and after that to face judgment". (Heb. 9:27)

Heaven on Earth

My soul craved heaven
I was stuck on death
As it being my only way out

Now coming to Alaska
I've seen heaven on earth
I can proclaim it with a shout

Away from complex people
I found a spot all by myself
Where I could lay
My painful burdens on the shelf

And spread out my hands
With palms facing up
With you, dear Jesus
Alone will I sup

Eating spiritual food
Of the smorgasbord type
I take in my fill
And ignore all the other hype

The drinking, the gambling,
The immoral sex, the thongs
So much of it too on this cruise

And yet, He gives to me
And in peace
I'm able to snooze

Because I've seen
A bit of heaven on earth
And through all this, dear Jesus
You show me my great worth

My great worth
That's what you have for me
I know that now
I feel surprisingly even more free

Free to commit
More deeply than ever
To life, to living,
For now and into forever.

The Cave of the Familiar

I notice within myself
That the familiar can become
A cave in which I live
A cave to which I succumb

I retreat to this cave
Despite a challenge to change
For this is home to me

It is so difficult
To move beyond it
And step out to see

To see what lies
Out there in the great unknown
I need to take steps of faith
This is what needs to be shown

If I am ever going to get
Beyond the safety of the cave
Lord, help me to grow

May I not retreat
But step out and be brave
And more of Your safety, Jesus to know.

Grace

As I follow me through my day
I sense myself going under
A mass of various emotions
I cannot keep track of

But grace holds me firm
Yes the anchor does hold
The miracle of salvation
The miracle of the Holy Spirit in me

Grace encompasses
Keeps me buoyant
When all around
Feels a crashing mess

I am so blessed
To have Jesus as my Savior
The One who works on my behalf

Please never leave me
With you inside me
I find I can truly laugh

At little mishaps
And things that happen
For You are Joy Incarnate

You free me
To find humor
Where I once found annoyance

You are the freeing God
Your grace abounds
Thank you for Your grace
With it, you hold me safe.

Substitute Saviors

"You've got to go to the lonesome valley,
No one can go there for you

You've got to go to the lonesome valley,
No one can go there for you"*

What do you lean on
Would it be sex,
Would it be a john?

Booze, other people, your own will
Do you rely at your core
On these things still?

What do you clutch
What is your crutch
To help you get by
Do you live in a lie?

Hatred, bitterness, rage
These can take us away
Hanging on to these
Crippled we will stay

Substitute saviors
Don't properly fill the hole
It's only through Jesus
That we become spiritually whole

For salvation, our best is yet unacceptable
We need to get forgiveness for sin
He needs to heal the state,
The condition we find ourselves in

Then, counseling, for deep healing
He may guide you to
As you work through tough emotions
And find His courage within you

For "you've got to go to the lonesome valley
No one can go there for you

You've got to go to the lonesome valley
No one can go there for you."

---

*   Taken from a song entitled, "Lonesome Valley" by
Fairfield Four of the *O Brother, Where Art Thou?*
soundtrack.

Breath

I have breath
I have been given breath
I can breathe
And feel free
To be just what I am

Lost at times
Sinner always
I am free to be me
Just me
Simple and true
I'm not anyone else
I'm not you

But you as well can be
Free and hopeful too
You can find peace
In what you are and do

I pray His peace
Upon your ways
With Him abide
And with you He stays*

Look in and up
And you will find
Hope everlasting
In body, soul and mind

Trust me today
'Cause I think I've found the way
To make life so worthwhile

I really do believe
If Him you receive
He will turn your frown to a smile.†

---

* Jesus's words: "Remain in me, and I will remain in you." (John 15:4a)
† "He [the Lord] has sent me [literally referring to a prophet] to bestow on them…the oil of gladness instead of mourning." (Isa. 61:3)

My Only Hope

They went from in my head
To in reality instead
Can't get away
From voices even today

For I have to hear
The words of those near
Secondhand conversations I do
Have to listen to

The nurses in the hall
Make such a racket for true
That I cannot find some
Quiet space for me or for you

A quiet little space
Is all I want to find
On God's green earth
Away from the daily grind...

...of the institution
No one can flourish here
I find I need something
Maybe rye, maybe beer

What I have is Someone
Jesus Christ, my Savior
To Him I'll cling
And pray all the more

Because He is Strength
And He is Hope
With Him alone
Is how I'll cope

Sometimes it seems
That He doesn't do that much
Doesn't take away
The pain or the suffering as such

But with it He molds
He strengthens He does
So go on dear Jesus, just help me

To seek You
All the time
For my only hope rests in Thee.

I Folded My Hands

I folded my hands to pray
I was in a prison
I reached to the Son
Who died and had risen

I asked him
His strength to give
To endure the bars
To help me live

The prison bars faded
In the light of Him
As the world around me
Grew strangely dim

All I could see
While being in the Light
Was Him and Him alone
It almost filled me with fright

For He is so real
Or has made Himself to be
Inside He is my Hope
Stay, dear Lord, always near to me.

Approaching Spring

The thaw is on, in more ways than one
On our streets as well as in our hearts
Trickle of activity as folk start
To shake off the winter blahs

Heavy coats are shed
Mittens and hats too
There is an aliveness in the air
For me and for you

Birds are singing and seem
To be flying more free
As the great weight of winter
Comes off them and me

For the world is awakening
From a slumber, a cold
It's putting on the new
And shedding the old

Wind in My Wings

Trees are coming to bud
And the sun again feels warm
Replacing with a lightness
The deep, dark snow storm

That was so ominous
Just a few short weeks ago
Now there are everywhere
Rivers of melting snow

I never did appreciate
Or feel quite so strong
The newness of the day
As it gets progressively long

For You mold something
Through the winter of our souls
That brings life and freedom anew

Please help me, Jesus
Understand Your ways
Or at least in all, see You.

Inaccessibility

Buildings I see
Inaccessibility
Stairs and more stairs
Adding to my cares

I approach my friend
And she does let me in
No steps to contend with
Smooth sailing with Him

For Jesus can help us overcome*
The barriers to our hearts
He's freely loving
Right from the start

And He helps us to be
In His love and feel free
Free to reach and take a stand
For justice for every woman, child and man

Yet His eternal nature is not
Totally accessible to the finite mind
For His ways, His thoughts
Are of a unique, one-of-a-kind[†]

But ask your questions
Your why ones too
In Him are still the answers
For both me and for you

And when you don't find answers
To all God says and does
Know that faith is the bridge
And in mystery still lies love.

---

* Jesus's words in John 16:33: "In this world you will have trouble. But take heart! I have overcome the world."

† "'For my thoughts are not your thoughts, neither are your ways my ways,' declares the Lord." (Isa. 55:8)

Secret Sin

Secret sin
Is there such a thing?

What do you do
Pornography, lust too?
What is needed is that
You get clean through and through

You need to go to Him
In repentance and holy fear*
He's the one to heal
He'll wipe every tear†

For He knows you
Through and through, He alone
To Him your sin
Is thoroughly known

It's your relationship
To Him that matters truly
You need to get right with Him
Then you can come to me

Confess your sins
One to another‡
Seek God first
Then go to your brother

Whatever it is
It grieves Him so
Won't you into His hands
I urge you, let it go?

---

* "The fear of the Lord is the beginning of wisdom."
(Ps. 111:10a)

† "The Sovereign Lord will wipe away the tears from
all faces." (Isa. 25:8); "And God will wipe away
every tear from their eyes." (Rev. 7:17c)

‡ "Therefore confess your sins to each other and pray
for each other so that you may be healed." (James
5:16)

A Little Plant

A little plant
All droopy and dry
Needs to be watered
Please do, please try

If you water it a lot
And do it all in one shot
It cannot absorb it for true

It needs a little bit
You need to water it
Many times, and often too

For the water is held
Better as time goes by
As you give little by little
Time after time after time

So please if you can
Throw it a line
Maybe you think little difference it'll make

But I assure you
Even this cactus
Grows with the little at a time I take.

Confined

Confined
In my body
And in my mind

For I want to fly
But for real, can I
With a heart full of fear?

It holds me back
And keeps me in black
As I shed tear upon tear

For I cannot overcome
This trial on my own
So give it to You, I will, Lord
For your faithfulness* You've shown…

…to me time and again
Certainly, it's in the Book
Help me to really focus
And have a good look

At your doing right
Helping sufferers pull through
Good is where You want me
Good You'll lead me to[†]

Maybe not
Of the physical kind
You might not take the suffering away

But You will sow
Treasures in my spirit
If, with You, I will stay[‡]

So, no matter how it looks
To the finite mind
Help me to rest in faith
When answers I cannot find

Lord, let us all break out
Of spiritual confinement
Make us who You want
Lord, do Your refinement.

* "Surely his salvation is near those who fear him, that his glory may dwell in our land. Love and faithfulness meet together; righteousness and peace kiss each other." (Ps. 85:9–10)

† "The Lord will indeed give what is good." (Ps. 85:12); "And we know that in all things God works for the good of those who love him, who have been called according to his purpose." (Rom. 8:28)

‡ Jesus's words in John 15:5: "I am the vine; you are the branches. If a man remains in me and I in him, he will bear much fruit; apart from me you can do nothing."

See Me Through

We turn away and sin
Deny Him access in
And His heart does feel the pain

Of separation
From the destination
To be like Jesus through the rain

The sting of sin
Produces a gap
Between me and a loving Savior

But as I repent
And plead for
His mercy all the more…

…He doesn't even blink
But accepts me right back
Forgiving as He goes

He's not like us
For we hold on
To anger and to our woes

What an awesome privilege
To call Jesus my friend
Please stay with me and see me through
Right to the very end.

Little Birds

Little birds
I see you fly
I used to be envious of this

I see you now
Land and hop
You're doing what I miss

I really am angry
My blood does boil
At Your allowing this
And bringing such toil

For I do not understand
Nor yet do I see
Why You have allowed
Such profound misery

To befall a little person
To befall a little girl
Though I know You can create
From a common grain of sand, a pearl

So weave your web
Lord, do your work
I'll stay right close to you

For I know
In You are
Still the answers for true.

In March of 2003, while I was living in the institution, we patients were restricted to the building for four weeks during the SARS outbreak. On the first day that I was allowed out, I went to sit in the garden and wrote this:

Freedom

When we think of freedom
We think of things like this
Walking on an open beach
Lovemaking sealed with a kiss

We think of horseback rides
Playground slides
Cars and bicycles too

We don't think of wheelchairs
And their enemies, the stairs
As being instruments of truth*

But there is a freedom
Of a spiritual kind
That brings hope and love anew

It grows in our hearts
In the midst of
The profound suffering we do

So please embrace
Your suffering for true
Jesus is trying to make
You more like Him, yes you.

---

* "To the Jews who had believed him, Jesus said, 'If you hold to my teaching you are really my disciples. Then you will know the truth, and the truth will set you free.'" (John 8:31–32)

A Pearl

Though you feel heavy
And burdened with care
And it's a long road
From here to there

Here in the intensity
Of the grief you feel
It's hard to believe you can
Be content* again for real

But, "my yoke is easy
And my burden is light"†
He is the Master
At making us bright

Bright stars for Him
It's always what He hopes
That you will take your trials
And do more than just cope

Rejoice in suffering[‡]
It seems absurd
Seems like the craziest
Thing I've ever heard

But rejoice we can
And rejoice we will
If, through our trials
We cleave to Him still

For it is hard
To love the very One
Who allowed the great sorrow
When all is said and done

But if we bring it to Jesus
We can watch as He makes
A pearl from the common grain
Of sand that He takes.

---

[*] Philippians 4:11b–13 (Paul in prison): "I have learned to be content whatever the circumstances. I know what it is to be in need and I know what it

is to have plenty. I have learned the secret of being content in any and every situation, whether well fed or hungry, whether living in plenty or in want. I can do everything through him who gives me strength."

† Jesus's words in Matt.11:28-30: "Come to me, all you who are weary and burdened, and I will give you rest. Take my yoke upon you and learn from me, for I am gentle and humble in heart, and you will find rest for your souls. For my yoke is easy and my burden is light."

‡ "And we rejoice in the hope of the glory of God. Not only so but we also rejoice in our sufferings, because we know that suffering produces perseverance; perseverance, character; and character, hope" (Rom. 5:2b–4); "But rejoice that you participate in the sufferings of Christ, so that you may be overjoyed when his glory is revealed." (1 Pet. 4:13)

Death Dew

Everyday
So hard
To push it away

Death dew
Collects
Each day anew

A fresh layer descends
On me this very day
Can't help but wish
That it would just have its way

Ready to go and find relief
From the endless barrage of pain
Cried so many tears of grief
Again and again and again

WIND IN MY WINGS

Tired of the struggle
And of the fight too
Rather wish sweet death
Would embrace me, would do

Do its work
For I've made my peace
With my Savior, Jesus
Now I seek relief

But wait, a work you are doing
You are helping me see
It's all about You
And not about me

You want to bring
Glory through the pain*
Draw others, and me to You

As folk reach out to me
They find they are
Discovering You, for true†

So please help me, Lord
Temptations to suicide to shun
For I will wait for Your time
Not my will, but Yours be done.‡

---

* My prayer. Can you make it yours?—"I want to know Christ and the power of his resurrection and the fellowship of sharing in his sufferings, becoming like him in his death, and so somehow, to attain to the resurrection from the dead." (Heb. 2:10; Phil. 3:10–11); "Dear friends, do not be surprised at the painful trial you are suffering, as though something strange were happening to you. But rejoice that you participate in the sufferings of Christ, so that you may be overjoyed when his glory is revealed." (1 Pet. 4:12–13)

† Jesus's words in Matt.25:40: "I tell you the truth, whatever you did for one of the least of these brothers of mine, you did for me."

‡ Matt.26:39 finds Jesus in His Garden of Gethsemane, praying, "My Father, if it is possible, may this cup be taken from me. Yet not as I will, but as you will." Can we follow the example of our dear Lord in this?

Keeping Up: A Prayer

"Dear Lord:
I find it hard
Just keeping up
Keeping in step with You
I really find hard to do

For time barrels on
So much to do
Can hardly find time
For me and for You

My quiet time it seems
Is the first to get
Squeezed out of my day

Oh Lord please help me
Discipline myself and
Let You have Your way

Your way with me
You long for me to be close

And develop spiritual intimacy

As Fernando Ortega sings,
'Don't let me
Come home a stranger.' Amen."

A Spiritual Weightlifter

Every day
Troubles
Troubles come
It's His way
Every day

I get so tired
I get so frustrated
When I think I've had enough
You heap on more

But help me to understand
That Your ways are not mine*
Help me go to You
Time after time after time

And help me to accept
Your divine help when you give it
So the horror of my sin
I don't have to relive it

Help me** be
A spiritual weightlifter
So I can in turn be for others
A spiritual hatelifter.

---

* "'For my thoughts are not your thoughts, neither are your ways my ways,' declares the Lord." (Isa.55:8)

† Joyce Meyer says sometimes we need to just repeat, "Lord, help me! Help me! Help me!"